ALL ABOUT

DINOSAURS

ALLOSAURUS

by

M

BookLife
PUBLISHING

©2021
BookLife Publishing Ltd.
King's Lynn
Norfolk PE30 4LS

A catalogue record for this book is available from the British Library.

ISBN: 978-1-83927-140-3

Written by:
Mignonne Gunasekara

Edited by:
Madeline Tyler

Designed by:
Amy Li

PHOTO CREDITS

Images are courtesy of Shutterstock.com. With thanks to Getty Images, Thinkstock Photo and iStockphoto.

Cover – Daniel Eskridge. Recurring – Nonchanon (rocks). 1 – wawritto. 2–3 – Catmando. 4–5 – Catmando. 6–7 – Michael Rosskothen. 8–9 – Jaroslav Moravcik, alice-photo, Dreamframer, Luis Louro, Macondo, Nine_Tomorrows. 10–11 – Herschel Hoffmeyer, Warpaint, Kostyantyn Ivanyshen. 12–13 – Digital Genetics, Herschel Hoffmeyer. 14–15 – Nekarius (wiki commons), The Hornbills Studio, Daniel Eskridge. 16–17 – Elenarts. 18–19 – Digital Genetics, David Herraez Calzada, Steve Bower, Herschel Hoffmeyer. 20–21 – Luis Molinero, Herschel Hoffmeyer. 22–23 – Catmando, Orla.

CONTENTS

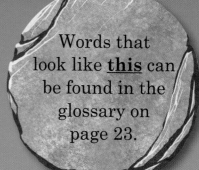

Words that look like **this** can be found in the glossary on page 23.

WHAT WERE DINOSAURS?

Dinosaurs were **reptiles** that lived on Earth for over 160 million years before they went **extinct**.

There were many different types of gigantic reptile. They lived both on land and in water – and some could even fly!

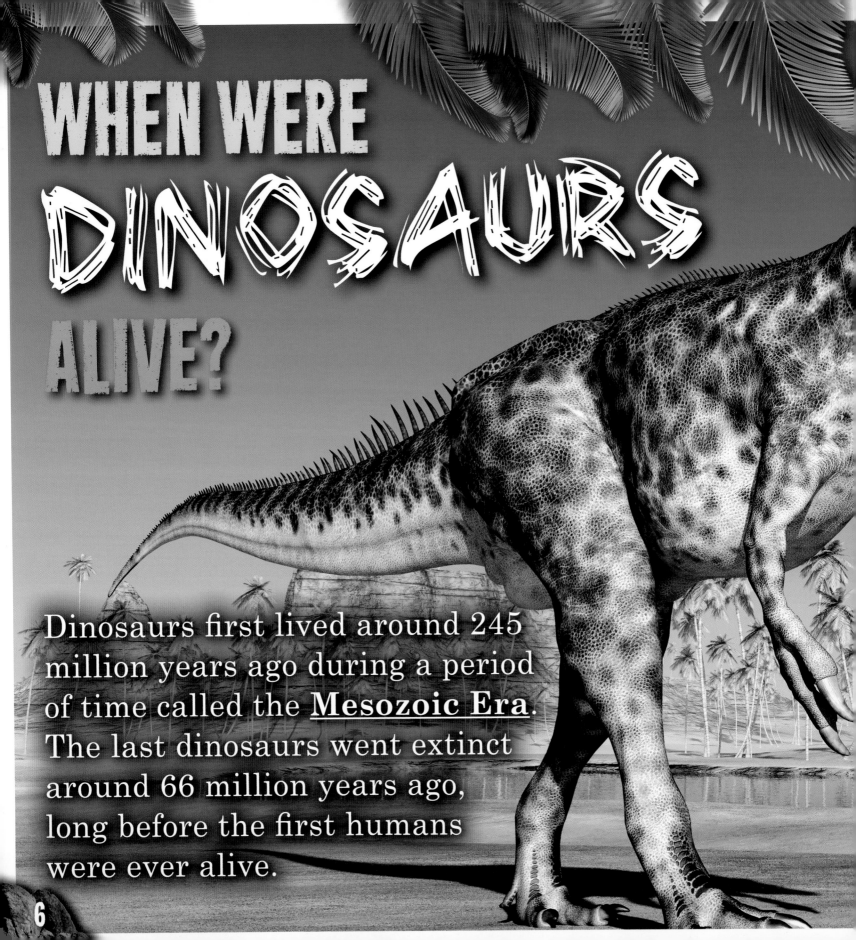

WHEN WERE DINOSAURS ALIVE?

Dinosaurs first lived around 245 million years ago during a period of time called the **Mesozoic Era**. The last dinosaurs went extinct around 66 million years ago, long before the first humans were ever alive.

Millions of years ago, all the land on Earth was together in one piece. But during the time of the dinosaurs, it slowly broke up into the different **continents** that we know today.

PANGEA

EURASIA

NORTH AMERICA

PACIFIC

SOUTH AMERICA

AFRICA

PACIFIC

INDIA

ANTARCTICA

WHEN ALL THE LAND ON EARTH WAS TOGETHER IN ONE PIECE, IT WAS CALLED PANGEA.

HOW DO WE KNOW...?

We know so much about dinosaurs thanks to the scientists, called palaeontologists (pay-lee-on-tol-uh-gists), who study them. They dig up <u>fossils</u> of dinosaurs to find out more about them.

FOSSILISED
DINOSAUR
EGGS

<u>Ammonite</u>
FOSSILS

Palaeontologists put together the bones they find to try to make full dinosaur skeletons. From these skeletons, palaeontologists can often work out the size and weight of a dinosaur. They can also find out information about what it ate from nearby fossils and fossilised poo.

PALAEONTOLOGISTS HAVE EVEN FOUND FOSSILISED EGGS AND FOOTPRINTS BELONGING TO DINOSAURS.

ALLOSAURUS SKELETON

DINOSAUR FOOTPRINT

ALLOSAURUS

Allosaurus was a large dinosaur that lived during the **Late Jurassic Period**. The first Allosaurus fossil was found in 1877 in Colorado, the US, by Othniel Charles Marsh. Many more Allosaurus fossils have been found since then.

NAME	Allosaurus (AL-oh-saw-russ)
LENGTH	12 metres
HEIGHT	4.5–5 metres
WEIGHT	2,000 kilograms
FOOD	**Carnivore**
WHEN IT LIVED	156–144 million years ago
HOW IT MOVED	Walked on two legs
WEAPONS	Sharp, **serrated** teeth

Allosaurus was not the largest **predator** around, but it was still really scary to other dinosaurs. Allosaurus attacked its **prey**, such as Apatosaurus, with its sharp teeth and hooked claws.

THE NAME 'ALLOSAURUS' MEANS 'DIFFERENT LIZARD' OR 'OTHER LIZARD'.

APATOSAURUS

ALLOSAURUS

WHAT DID ALLOSAURUS LOOK LIKE?

SMALL HORNS

LARGE SKULL

SHARP TEETH

Allosaurus had a skull that was very large for its body. Its skull had bony ridges that ran from the nose up towards the eyes, where they turned into small horns.

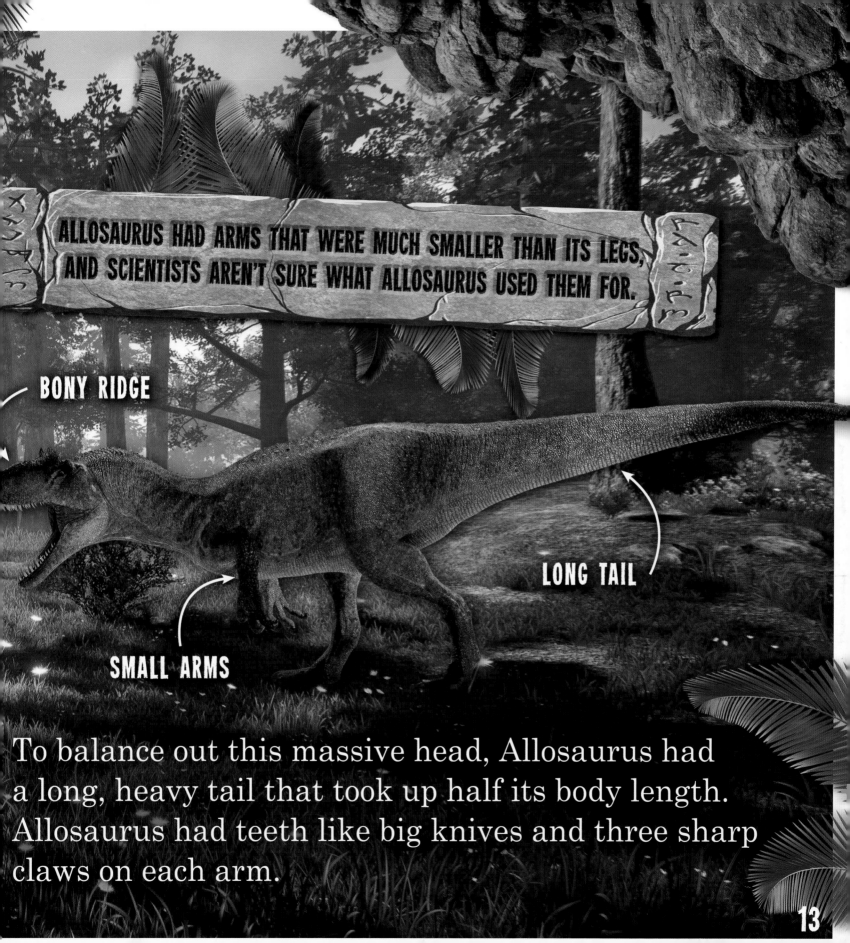

ALLOSAURUS HAD ARMS THAT WERE MUCH SMALLER THAN ITS LEGS, AND SCIENTISTS AREN'T SURE WHAT ALLOSAURUS USED THEM FOR.

BONY RIDGE

LONG TAIL

SMALL ARMS

To balance out this massive head, Allosaurus had a long, heavy tail that took up half its body length. Allosaurus had teeth like big knives and three sharp claws on each arm.

WHERE DID ALLOSAURUS LIVE?

Many Allosaurus fossils have been found in the western US in what is now Wyoming, Colorado and Utah. Many fossils have been found in the Cleveland-Lloyd Quarry and the Garden Park Quarry.

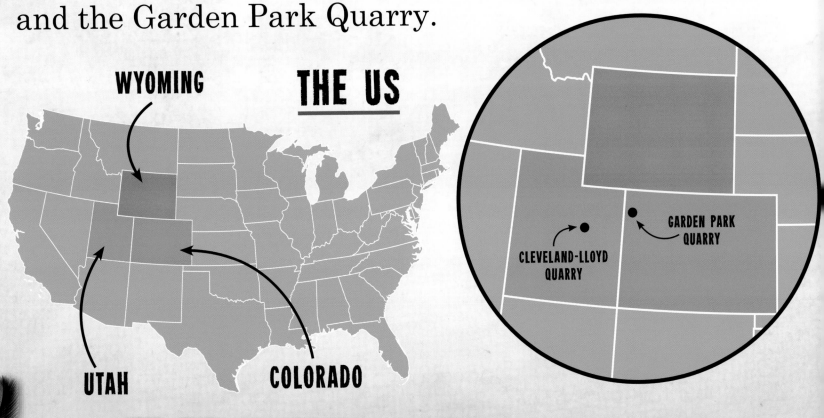

THE US

WYOMING

UTAH

COLORADO

GARDEN PARK QUARRY

CLEVELAND-LLOYD QUARRY

A QUARRY IS A DEEP PIT FROM WHICH MATERIALS CAN BE REMOVED. HERE, THE MATERIAL WAS DINOSAUR FOSSILS!

A lot of Allosaurus fossils have been found in the Morrison Formation in the US and the Lourinhã Formation in Portugal. These formations are rock beds that contain lots of fossils from throughout the years.

LOURINHÃ FORMATION, PORTUGAL

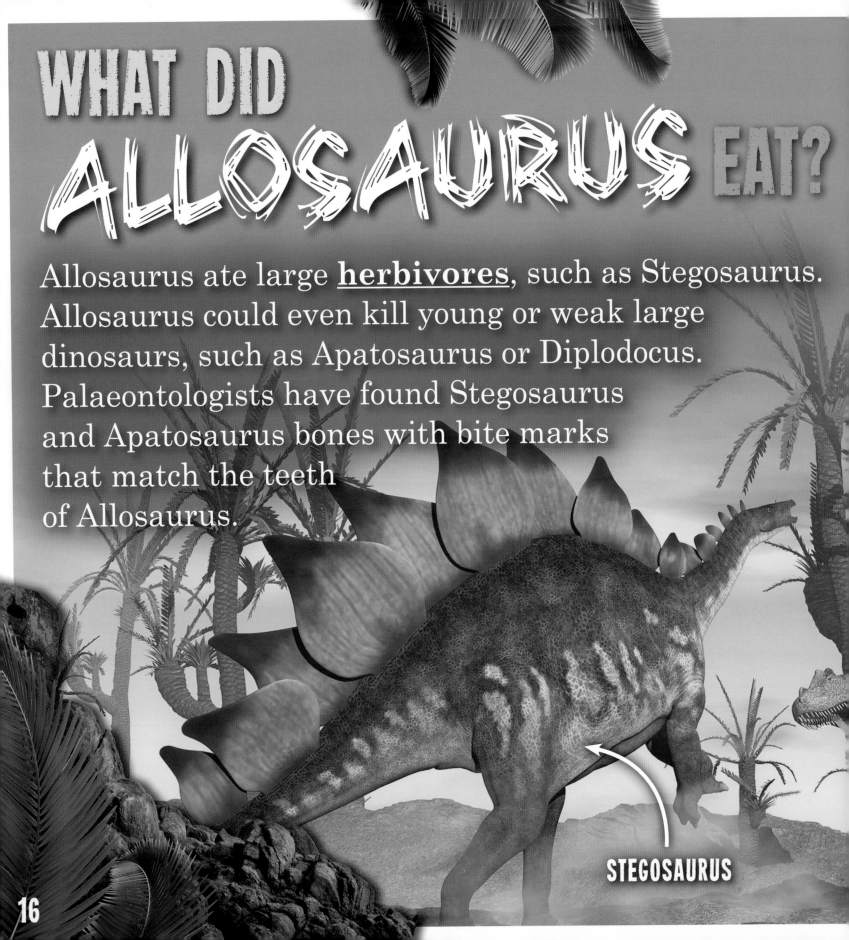

WHAT DID ALLOSAURUS EAT?

Allosaurus ate large **herbivores**, such as Stegosaurus. Allosaurus could even kill young or weak large dinosaurs, such as Apatosaurus or Diplodocus. Palaeontologists have found Stegosaurus and Apatosaurus bones with bite marks that match the teeth of Allosaurus.

STEGOSAURUS

As well as being a hunter, Allosaurus was probably also a **scavenger**. Scientists can't agree on whether Allosaurus hunted alone like tigers, or whether they attacked healthy large dinosaurs such as Apatosaurus in small groups.

ALLOSAURUS

ALLOSAURUS TEETH MARKS HAVE ALSO BEEN FOUND ON THE BONES OF... OTHER ALLOSAURUS!

DID ALLOSAURUS HAVE THE BIGGEST TEETH?

ALLOSAURUS

ALLOSAURUS SKULL

Allosaurus had teeth that were sharp and had serrated edges, making them perfect for slicing meat. Allosaurus was very rough when it ate, so its teeth probably fell out easily and would need to be replaced with new teeth.

TYRANNOSAURUS
SKULL

TYRANNOSAURUS

Allosaurus had teeth that
were just over ten centimetres
long and curved inwards so prey
couldn't run away. Tyrannosaurus had the
biggest teeth, which were up to 15 centimetres long!

FACTS ABOUT
ALLOSAURUS

It is thought that Allosaurus could run faster than 33 kilometres per hour.

LONG TAIL

ALLOSAURUS POO HAS BEEN FOUND THAT WAS 1.52 METRES LONG AND 10.2 CENTIMETRES THICK!

Allosaurus had a bite that was weak for how large its skull was, but Allosaurus could open its jaws really wide. This makes some palaeontologists think Allosaurus used its sharp teeth to slash at its prey, not chomp.

HORNS

BONY RIDGE

SERRATED TEETH

SMALL ARMS

THREE TOES

WHERE IS ALLOSAURUS?

Can you find Allosaurus hiding in this scene?

The answer can be found on page 24.

GLOSSARY

ammonite — a type of sea creature with flat, spiral shells that no longer exists

carnivore — an animal that eats other animals, instead of plants

continents — large areas of land that are made up of many countries

extinct — no longer existing

fossils — parts or traces of plants and animals from a long time ago that have been kept in good condition inside rocks

herbivores — animals that only eat plants

Late Jurassic Period — the period of time between 164 and 145 million years ago

Mesozoic Era — the period of time between 250 and 66 million years ago, when dinosaurs lived

predator — an animal that hunts other animals for food

prey — animals that are hunted by other animals for food

reptiles — cold-blooded animals that are usually covered in scales

scavenger — an animal that eats dead animals that they have not killed themselves

serrated — has a row of sharp points along the edge

INDEX